3 1994 00939 0219

SA

D0605104

SA

1944

MOLLY'S CRAFT BOOK

*A Look at
Crafts from the
Past with Projects
You Can Make Today*

J 745.5 MOL

Molly's craft book

$5.95
 31994009390219

PLEASANT COMPANY PUBLICATIONS

Published by Pleasant Company Publications
© Copyright 1994 by Pleasant Company
All rights reserved. No part of this book may be used or reproduced
in any manner whatsoever without written permission except in the
case of brief quotations embodied in critical articles and reviews.
For information, address: Book Editor, Pleasant Company Publications,
8400 Fairway Place, P.O. Box 620998, Middleton, WI 53562.

First Edition.
Printed in the United States of America.
97 98 99 WCR 10 9 8 7

The American Girls Collection® and Molly McIntire®
are registered trademarks of Pleasant Company.

PICTURE CREDITS
The following individuals and organizations have generously
given permission to reprint illustrations in this book:
Page 1—AP/Wide World Photos; 4—From the book *Home Front, U.S.A.*,
by A. A. Hoehling; 5—National Archives; 9—Oregon Historical Society;
11—Jack Westhead, Plainfield, IN; 13—Joanne Kash, Holly Hill, FL; 15—Chicago
Historical Society, ICHi-22567 (bottom); 19—Peter Stackpole, LIFE Magazine © Time
Warner Inc.; 20—Archive Photos/Lambert; 21—Peter Stackpole, LIFE Magazine ©
Time Warner Inc., Set #28195; 23—Frank Scherschel-Fritz Henle, Black Star;
25—Courtesy Harry N. Abrams, Inc., New York (Scottie button); Courtesy:
Margaret Suckley; 27—State Historical Society of Wisconsin; 29—Hazel Carew from
Monkmeyer Press Photo Service; 31—Illustration from the Montgomery Ward
Spring/Summer 1943 Catalog courtesy Montgomery Ward & Co., Chicago (bottom);
33—Milton Bradley Company, 1944; 34—State Historical Society of Wisconsin;
36, 37—Library of Congress; 39—Permission to use granted by
Brown Group, Inc., St. Louis, MO; 40—Joyce Witovic, Newport, NH;
41—Courtesy Harry N. Abrams, Inc., New York.

Edited by Jodi Evert
Written by Rebecca Sample Bernstein and Jodi Evert
Designed and Art Directed by Jane S. Varda
Produced by Karen Bennett, Laura Paulini, and Pat Tuchscherer
Cover Illustration by Nick Backes
Inside Illustration by Geri Strigenz Bourget
Photography by Mark Salisbury
Historical and Picture Research by Polly Athan,
Rebecca Sample Bernstein, Jodi Evert, and Doreen Smith
Crafts Made by Jean doPico, Kristi Jacobek, and June Pratt
Craft Testing Coordinated by Jean doPico
Prop Research by Leslie Cakora

All the instructions in this book have been tested by both children and adults.
Results from their testing were incorporated into this book. Nonetheless, all
recommendations and suggestions are made without any guarantees on the part of
Pleasant Company Publications. Because of differing tools, materials, conditions, and
individual skills, the publisher disclaims liability for any injuries, losses, or other
damages that may result from using the information in this book.

Library of Congress Cataloging-in-Publication Data

Evert, Jodi.
Molly's craft book : a look at crafts from the past with projects you can make today /
[edited by Jodi Evert ; written by Jodi Evert and Rebecca Sample Bernstein ; inside
illustration by Geri Strigenz Bourget ; photography by Mark Salisbury].
p. cm.
ISBN 1-56247-118-X
1. Handicraft—Juvenile literature. 2. United States—Social life and customs—
1918-1945—Juvenile literature. [1. Handicraft.
2. United States—Social life and customs—1918-1945.]
I. Bernstein, Rebecca Sample. II. Bourget, Geri Strigenz, ill.
III. Salisbury, Mark, ill. IV. Title.
TT171.E84   1994   745.5—dc20   94-17550   CIP   AC

CONTENTS

S pecial thanks to all the children and adults who tested the crafts and gave us their valuable comments:

Kimberly Beck and her mother Dorothy Beck
Amie Bergquist and her mother Tari Bergquist
Nina Borokhim and her mother Barbara Borokhim
Sara Brozek and her mother Diane Brozek
Jennifer Fox and her mother Barbara Fox
Lindsey Foy and her mother Susan Foy
Angela Fraser and her mother Janet Wells
Janessa Graves and her mother Debra Graves
Ellen Hauschen and her father Paul Hauschen
Elise Hein and her mother Ruth Hoffman Hein
Jana Hicks and her mother Shelly Hicks
Emily and Sarah Holcomb and their mother Melissa Holcomb
Emily Holler and her mother Lana Holler
Andrew and Lauren Johnson and their mother Christine Johnson
Michael Kittle and his mother Denise Kittle
Mallory Kroon and her mother Kelly Kroon
Melissa Lindsay and her mother Patty Lindsay
Courtney Masbruch and her mother Dawn Masbruch
Katie Monk and her mother Jan Monk
Meredith Newlin and her mother Karen Watson-Newlin
Samantha Jo Oscar and her mother Sue Oscar
Jillian Parish and her mother Sally Parish
Megan Petrie and her mother Mary Petrie
Clarlie Rasmussen and her mother Faye Rasmussen
Mollie Rostad and her mother Genie Campbell
Maria Schmitz and her mother Jean Tretow-Schmitz
Katrina Schroeder and her mother Orange Schroeder
Kelly Sloan and her mother Nancy Sloan
Heidi Tiefenthaler and her mother Liz Tiefenthaler
Kelly Toltzien and her mother Paula Toltzien
Alexandra Vailas and her mother Laura Vailas
Briony Varda and her mother Jane Varda
Katherine Vater and her mother Barbara Vater
Megan Verhelst and her mother Mary Verhelst
Rachel Vitense and her mother Mary Vitense
Lindsay Wadleigh and her mother Barbara Wadleigh
Kari Lynn Walter and her mother Linda Walter
Caitlin Wichlacz and her mother Jacqueline Wichlacz
Stephanie Winter and her mother Jackie Winter
Amy Wittrock and her mother Beverly Wittrock-Zierbarth
Rowena Zirbel and her mother Jodi Zirbel

CRAFTS FROM THE PAST

During World War Two, thousands of American soldiers were fighting in faraway lands. Their families were fighting, too—on America's home front.

Children like Molly helped the war effort by collecting metal and other materials needed for war

Boy collecting scrap metal.

equipment. They took care of their clothes and toys because they had to last. During World War Two, most clothing factories made uniforms for soldiers instead of clothes for children, and toy factories needed to make war equipment.

But children on the home front were clever.

MOLLY ★ 1944

Molly McIntire was a lively schemer and dreamer living on America's home front during World War Two. She grew up at a time when America was hardworking and hopeful, patriotic and proud.

They learned how to make their own toys and games from scraps they found around their houses—bits of fabric and paper, old jars and bottles, string, and erasers. They used sticks, tin cans, and even old gardening gloves to play games like stickball, kick-the-can, and a beanbag toss game called Handshake.

Children like Molly made practical things, too, such as bookmarks, handkerchiefs, and photo holders. These projects were useful at home and at school, and children sent them to soldiers and gave them as gifts to family members.

Learning how and why crafts were made long ago will help you understand what it was like to grow up the way Molly did. Making the crafts she might have made will bring history alive for you today.

CRAFT TIPS

This list of tips gives you some hints about creating the crafts in this book. But this is the most important tip: **work with an adult**. The best thing about these crafts is the fun you will have making them together.

1. Choose a time that suits you and the adult who's working with you, so that you will both enjoy making crafts together.

2. You can find most of the materials listed in this book in your home or at craft and fabric stores. If an item in the materials list is starred (*), look at the bottom of the list to find out where you can get it.

3. If you don't have something you need or can't find it at the store, think of something similar you could use. You might just think of something that works even better!

4. Read the instructions for a craft all the way through before you start it. Look at the pictures. They will help you understand the steps.

5. If there's a step that doesn't make sense to you, try it out with a piece of scrap paper or fabric first. Sometimes acting it out helps.

6. Select a good work area for your craft project. Pick a place that has plenty of light and is out of reach of pets and younger brothers and sisters.

PAINTS AND BRUSHES

*You'll use water-based, or **acrylic**, paints to make some of the crafts in this book. Here are a few hints for using paints and brushes:*

★ *Don't dip your brush into the paint bottle. Squeeze a little paint onto newspaper or a paper plate.*

★ *Have a bowl of water handy to clean the brush each time you change colors.*

★ *Make sure one color is dry before adding another.*

★ *Clean your brush with soap and water and let it dry before you put it away.*

7. Wear an apron, tie back your hair, and roll up your sleeves. Cover your work area with newspapers and gather all the materials you will need before you start.

8. It pays to be careful. Be sure to get an adult's help when the instructions tell you to. Have an adult help you use tools properly. Don't use the stove or oven without an adult's permission.

9. Pay attention when using sharp knives and scissors so you don't cut your fingers! Remember—good, sharp knives and scissors are safer and easier to use than dull ones.

10. To prevent spills, put the covers back on containers tightly. If you do spill, clean it up right away.

11. If your craft doesn't turn out exactly like the picture in the book, that's terrific! The pictures are there just to give you ideas. Crafts become more meaningful when you add your own personal touch.

12. Cleanup is part of making crafts, too. Leave your work area as clean as you found it. Wash and dry dishes, trays, and tabletops. Sweep the floor. Throw away the garbage.

THREADING A NEEDLE

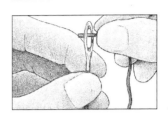

1. Wet the tip of the thread in your mouth. Then push the tip of the thread through the eye of the needle.

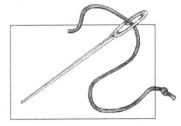

2. Pull about 5 inches of the thread through the needle. Then tie a double knot near the end of the long tail of thread.

STAR-SPANGLED HANDICRAFTS

A patriotic parade.

Americans on the home front knew it was important to show their support for soldiers fighting in the war. They did this in many ways. They made food packages to send overseas and rolled bandages for the Red Cross. And on patriotic holidays like the Fourth of July, Americans showed their pride in their country and their soldiers with music, fireworks, and patriotic parades.

On Molly's street, the Fourth of July meant a neighborhood celebration. Everyone pitched in to help. Mrs. Silvano was in charge of refreshments and decorations. Mr. Koloski organized the games and fireworks. And Molly took the lead in planning the star-spangled children's parade.

During the week before the Fourth of July, Molly invited all the neighborhood children over to her backyard for a parade planning party. They spent the day decorating their bikes, scooters, and doll buggies with red, white, and blue streamers and 48-star flags. They made pinwheels decorated with gold stars, and star whirlers to twirl during the parade. Even their parade posters were stamped with stars.

At noon on the Fourth of July, all the neighbors lined the street to watch the parade. Children on bikes led the parade, honking their horns. Then came the doll buggy brigade and the scooter patrol. Next came the children's band, which played patriotic songs by blowing on kazoos and banging on pots and pans. For the grand finale, Molly and her friends Linda and Susan roller-skated past their cheering neighbors, with star whirlers waving and pinwheels spinning in the breeze.

STAR-SPANGLED HANDICRAFTS

Star Whirler

•

Patriotic Pinwheel

•

Star-Stamp Stationery

48-STAR FLAG

During World War Two, Americans flew flags everywhere to show their patriotism. In 1944, the flag had 48 stars. That flag was used longer than any other—from 1912 until 1959, when Alaska and Hawaii became the 49th and 50th states.

STAR WHIRLER

Give these glittery stars a twirl!

MATERIALS

Foam paintbrush, 1 inch wide
Acrylic paints, any colors
3-foot wooden dowel, $\frac{1}{2}$ inch wide
Small artist's paintbrush
Pencil
Sheet of tracing paper
Sheet of newspaper
3 sheets of construction paper, any colors
Scissors
White glue
3 ribbons, each 3 feet long
Glitter

DIRECTIONS

1. Use the foam paintbrush to paint a base color onto the dowel.

2. When the base coat is dry, use the artist's paintbrush to add designs to the dowel.

3. To make a star streamer, use a pencil to trace the star pattern shown on page 42 onto tracing paper twice. Don't cut out the stars.

4. Place the sheet of tracing paper onto newspaper, design side down. Use the side of the pencil to color over the lines on the back of each star pattern.

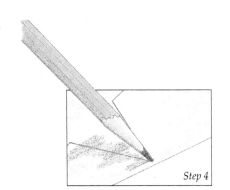

Step 4

5. Place the tracing paper on top of a sheet of construction paper, design side up. Then draw over the lines of the patterns, pressing firmly.

6. Lift up the tracing paper. The pencil markings from the back of the tracing paper will come off where you traced. Cut out the stars.

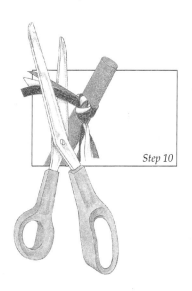
Step 6

7. Glue a ribbon to 1 of the stars as shown. Then glue the other star on top. Make 2 more star streamers in the same way.

Step 7

8. To decorate your stars, squeeze glue designs onto 1 side of each star. Use a light touch— a little glue goes a long way! Then sprinkle glitter over the glue.

9. When the glue is dry, decorate the other side of each star.

10. After the glue has dried, gather the ends of all 3 ribbons together. Then tie them in a tight double knot around the dowel. Trim off the extra tails of ribbon, and whirl your stars! ★

Step 10

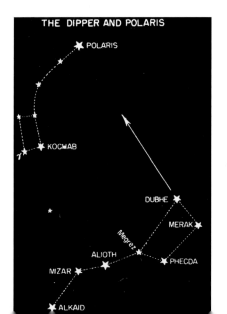

THE DIPPER AND POLARIS

POLARIS
KOCHAB
DUBHE
MERAK
Megrez
ALIOTH
PHECDA
MIZAR
ALKAID

GUIDING STARS

Fighting men weren't always told where they were being sent to fight. They weren't told because enemy spies might be among them, trying to overhear American plans. So on the decks of their ships at night, sailors and soldiers looked for constellations to figure out where they were going. A **constellation** *is a group of stars that form a shape, like the Big Dipper.*

PATRIOTIC PINWHEEL

Watch your pinwheel spin in the breeze, or twirl yourself to make it whirl!

MATERIALS

Pencil
Ruler
Piece of construction paper, 5 inches square
Piece of tracing paper, 3 inches square
Scissors
White glue
Small plastic bead
Straight pin, 1 inch long *(Pleat pins work well.)*
Wooden bead, about $1/2$ inch wide
Unsharpened pencil with eraser
Gold foil stars*

*Available in the school supplies section of department stores.

DIRECTIONS

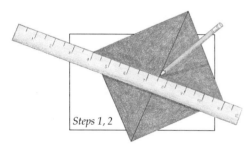

Steps 1, 2

1. Use the pencil and ruler to draw a line from the top right corner of the construction paper to the bottom left corner.

2. Then draw a line from the top left corner to the bottom right corner.

3. Trace the circle shown on page 43 onto tracing paper. Mark the dot in the center of the circle, too.

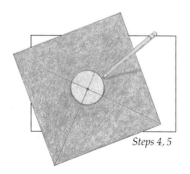

Steps 4, 5

4. Carefully cut out the circle from the tracing paper. Place it in the middle of the construction paper square, with the dot centered over the place where the lines cross.

5. Trace around the circle. Then set the circle aside.

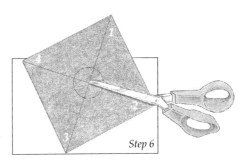

6. Number the corners of the square as shown. Starting at the corners, cut along the pencil lines to the edge of the circle.

Step 6

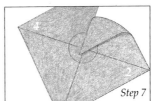

7. Put a small dot of glue in the center of the circle. Then fold corner 1 to the center. Hold the corner down for a few seconds, until it stays down by itself.

Step 7

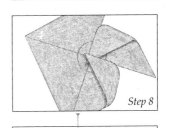

8. Glue corner 2 on top of corner 1. The corners should overlap a little. Continue gluing the other corners to the center in the same way.

Step 8

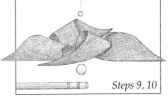

9. Slip the small plastic bead onto the straight pin, and then stick the pin all the way through the center of the pinwheel.

Steps 9, 10

10. Slip the wooden bead onto the pin. Push the pin into the eraser of the pencil. Make sure the point of the pin doesn't poke through the eraser. Decorate your pinwheel with gold foil stars. ★

WARTIME TOYS

In 1944, children often donated their metal toys to the war effort. The toys were melted down to make war supplies. Instead of playing with metal toys, many children used simple materials like paper to make their own puppets and airplanes, and they turned cardboard boxes into houses or spaceships, just as children do today.

STAR-STAMP STATIONERY

Make your very own star-spangled stationery!

MATERIALS

Pencil
Piece of tracing paper, 2 inches square
Sheet of newspaper
Piece of poster board, 2 inches square
Scissors
Thumbtack
Artgum eraser, 2 inches long, 1 inch wide, and 1 inch tall
Ballpoint pen
Manicure stick*
Stamp pad
Plain pieces of writing paper
Available in the cosmetics section of department stores.

DIRECTIONS

1. To make a stamp, use the pencil to trace the star pattern shown on page 43 onto the tracing paper. Don't cut out the star.

2. Place the piece of tracing paper onto a sheet of newspaper, design side down. Use the side of the pencil to color over the lines on the back side of the pattern.

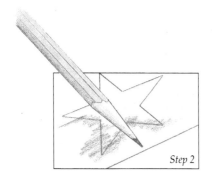

Step 2

3. Place the tracing paper on top of the piece of poster board, design side up. Then draw over the lines of the pattern, pressing firmly.

4. Lift up the tracing paper. The pencil markings from the back of the tracing paper will come off where you traced. Cut out the star.

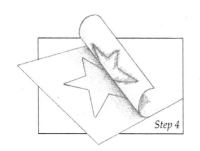

Step 4

5. Tack the star pattern to 1 end of the eraser. Use the pen to trace around the star, and then unpin the pattern.

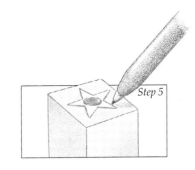

6. Cut around the star with the pointed end of the manicure stick. Cut just outside the pen lines, not directly on them.

7. Then use the manicure stick to carve away the background around the star bit by bit.

8. Press your star stamp onto the stamp pad. Then stamp plain pieces of writing paper to make your own stationery.

9. You can also carve another design in the other end of the eraser to get 2 stamps in 1! ★

BLUE AND GOLD STARS

During World War Two, a family who had a relative fighting in the military hung a blue star in a window or on the front door. If the relative was killed, the family replaced the blue star with a gold star. Women whose sons were killed in the war were known as Gold Star Mothers.

"V Is for Victory"

During World War Two, the word *victory* and the letter *V* were everywhere, reminding Americans that even if they weren't soldiers, they could still do their part to work for victory.

Many families worked for victory by raising their own vegetables in Victory gardens. The more vegetables they ate fresh from their gardens, the more canned vegetables could be sent to soldiers fighting overseas. Fresh vegetables didn't ship well—they got crushed or turned bad too quickly.

Americans drove at a "victory speed limit" of 35 miles per hour to keep their tires from wearing out. They couldn't get new tires for their cars because factories needed the rubber to make war supplies like life rafts and gas masks. And in 1943, there was even a "victory model" alarm clock to help workers get to their war jobs on time.

Americans wrote to soldiers on V-Mail forms, which were photographed onto rolls of film, shipped overseas, and printed out for soldiers to read. The film took up less room in mailbags than regular letters did. People also hummed the first four notes of Beethoven's Fifth Symphony (da-da-da-dummm). The notes sounded like Morse code for the letter *V* (dot-dot-dot-dash)!

On September 2, 1945, America celebrated the biggest victory of them all—victory over Japan, which was celebrated on "V-J Day." Finally, the war was over! Church bells rang, sirens sounded, and parties and parades took place in the streets. Children like Molly made confetti by shredding old phone books, threw V-J Day parachutes into the air, and made as much noise as they could by blowing whistles and horns, ringing bells, and banging pots and pans. V-J Day was nothing to keep quiet about!

"V Is for Victory"

★

Victory Garden in a Jar

•

V-Stitch Handkerchief

•

V-J Day Parachute

V-Pins

Women who had loved ones at war often wore "V for Victory" pins, like those pictured at left, to show how proud they were of their soldiers. Some pins were simple V shapes, while others were fancier, with patriotic images of eagles or soldiers as part of the design.

VICTORY GARDEN IN A JAR

Grow your very own Victory garden right on a windowsill.

MATERIALS

Widemouthed glass jar with metal or cork lid
Spoon
1 cup of gravel*
2 cups of potting soil*
Small bowl
Water in a small spray bottle
1/2 tablespoon herb seeds *(Chives or parsley work well.)**
Hammer and nail *(needed only if your jar has a metal lid)*
Tiny toy houses, people, and animals *(optional)*
Tongs
Scissors
Available at garden stores.

DIRECTIONS

1. If your jar has round sides, place it upright onto the table. If your jar has flat sides, you can lay it on its side. Spoon the gravel into the jar until the gravel is 1/4 inch deep.

2. Put the potting soil into the small bowl. Stir the soil and mist it with water until it is damp.

3. Spoon the soil into the jar until the soil is 1 inch deep.

4. Sprinkle the herb seeds into the jar, and then lightly cover them with soil.

5. If your jar has a metal lid, ask an adult to help you hammer 5 air holes into it. If your jar has a cork lid, no air holes are needed.

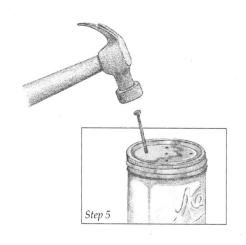

Step 5

6. Close the jar with the lid and set it in a sunny window.

7. Check the soil each day. When your garden is dry, mist it with water.

8. When your seeds begin to sprout, decorate your garden with tiny toy houses, people, and animals.

9. To harvest your herbs, hold each leaf with tongs, and then cut off the leaf with scissors. Use your herbs to season soups, salads, and other foods. ★

HERBS ON THE HOME FRONT

During World War Two, spices like pepper were in short supply in the United States because of the fighting in India and other countries where the spices were grown. So home-front families learned to use herbs they could grow themselves, like basil and parsley, to season their food.

GARDENING FOR VICTORY

Since farmers were busy growing food for the troops, Americans began growing their own vegetables. Victory gardens sprouted everywhere—in backyards, schoolyards, parking lots, and even in a zoo in Oregon! Victory gardens produced nearly half of the vegetables home-front families ate.

V-STITCH HANDKERCHIEF

This handkerchief is edged with the Victory V-stitch!

MATERIALS

Scissors
Embroidery floss, any color
Embroidery needle
White handkerchief, washed and ironed
Ruler
Fabric pen with disappearing ink

DIRECTIONS

1. Cut an 18-inch piece of embroidery floss. The floss is made up of 6 strands. When you embroider, you need only 2 strands. Separate 2 strands.

2. Thread the needle with the 2 strands. Tie a double knot near the other end of the floss.

3. Use the V-stitch to make a pretty border around your handkerchief. Begin in the top right corner of the handkerchief, 1/4 inch from each edge. This will be point A.

4. Bring the needle up at A, and then go down at B.

5. Then bring the needle up at C and go down at D. Keep stitching!

6. When you run out of floss, tie a knot under the fabric, close to your last stitch. Cut off the extra thread. Then begin stitching again.

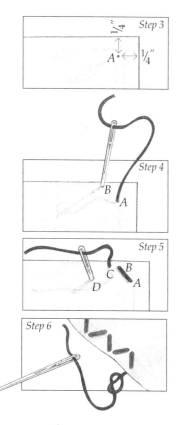

7. For a finishing touch, use the fabric pen to write your initials in 1 corner. If you're not happy with them, try again in another corner. The ink will disappear in a few days.

8. Backstitch your initials. To backstitch, come up at A and go down at B.

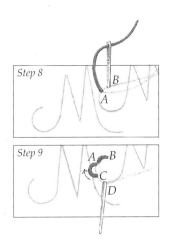

Step 8

Step 9

9. Come up at C. Then go down at A and come up at D. Keep stitching!

10. When you've finished stitching your initials, your handkerchief is complete! ★

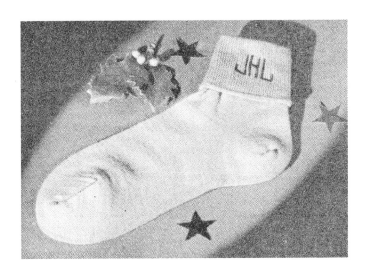

MONOGRAMS

*A **monogram** is a design made with the initials of a person's name. In Molly's day, it was popular to monogram sweaters, blouses, towels, handkerchiefs, and even socks!*

V-J DAY PARACHUTE

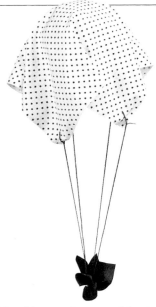

Use this parachute to celebrate
V-J Day on September 2, or anytime
you're feeling victorious!

MATERIALS

Piece of fabric, 15 inches square
Ruler
Fabric pen or pencil
Scissors
4 pieces of string, each 15 inches long
Piece of fabric, 5 inches square
Small stone, 1 inch wide
Rubber band

DIRECTIONS

1. Lay the 15-inch fabric square onto a table with the *right side*, or front side, facing up.

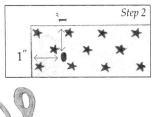
Step 2

2. At the upper left corner, measure 1 inch in from the side and 1 inch down from the top. Mark a small dot on that spot.

3. Mark a small dot in the other 3 corners in the same way.

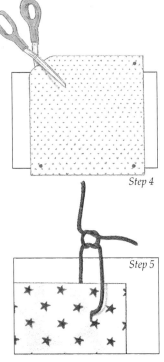
Step 4

4. Cut a small slit on each marked dot. To cut a slit, fold in the edge of the fabric so that a dot shows on the fold. Then cut a small slit on the dot.

Step 5

5. Thread a string through 1 of the slits. Make a loop, and then tie the string in a double knot.

6. Thread pieces of string through the rest of the slits in the same way.

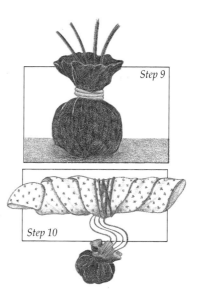

7. Lay the 5-inch square of fabric onto the table, with the *wrong side*, or back side, facing up. Then lay the ends of the strings across the 5-inch fabric square as shown.

8. Place the stone on top of the strings.

9. Fold the cloth around the stone to form a small pouch. Close the pouch with the rubber band.

10. Take your parachute outside and roll it up as shown. Then toss it high into the air. The parachute will open as it floats back down to the ground!   ★

A PARACHUTE WEDDING GOWN!

During the war, parachutes carried troops and supplies into hard-to-reach places. Parachutes could also save soldiers' lives if their planes were hit in battle. One woman was so grateful that a parachute saved the life of her fiancé that she made her wedding dress out of it!

A STITCH IN TIME

Woman working in factory.

During World War Two, many women worked outside their homes for the first time. Some women worked in factories stitching flags, uniforms, and parachutes. Other women made airplanes, tanks, and jeeps.

Some people didn't think women should work outside their homes. But when men left their jobs to fight in the war, factories needed workers. Even though women did the same work as men, they earned an average of $40 per week, which was only half of what men made.

In 1944, fabric for dresses and other non-military clothes was strictly limited so that more fabric could be used for soldiers' uniforms. To save fabric, dressmakers shortened hems on skirts and dresses and stopped adding "extras" such as cuffs, hoods, and ruffles. Even zippers and elastic were restricted because metal and rubber were needed to make war supplies. Instead, buttons were used to keep clothes in place—even on underwear!

Women worked at home, too, cooking, cleaning, and sometimes making clothes for their children. Both boys and girls loved to wear military outfits. Some mothers made sailor suits, nurses' capes, and WAC (Women's Army Corps) uniforms for their children.

Children like Molly helped "stitch for victory." They sewed photo holders and bookmarks to send to soldiers. Molly and her friends even knitted a blanket to send to an army hospital. The Red Cross had a "Knittin' for Britain" project, too. Each volunteer knitted a scarf to keep a soldier warm during the cold English winter. One girl knitted a scarf that was long enough to wrap around a soldier's whole body!

A STITCH IN TIME

Apple Potholder

•

Scottie Bookmark

•

Photo Holder

APPLE POTHOLDER

*Make a fun, fruity potholder
for your kitchen!*

MATERIALS

Pencil
2 sheets of tracing paper
Scissors
Straight pins
2 pieces of red felt, each 8 inches square
Piece of green felt, 4 inches square
Thread *(red and green)*
Needle
Circle of polyester batting, 5$\frac{1}{2}$ inches wide *(Use a
  small plate as a cutting guide.)*
Piece of brown yarn, 5 inches long

DIRECTIONS

1. Use the pencil to trace the apple and leaf
patterns shown on page 44 onto tracing paper
twice each, and then cut them out.

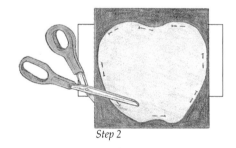

Step 2

2. Pin 1 apple pattern to each piece of red felt,
and then cut out the apple shapes. Unpin
the patterns.

3. Pin both leaf patterns onto the green felt, and
then cut out the leaves. Unpin the patterns.

4. Pin the felt leaves onto 1 of the felt apple
shapes.

5. Cut an 18-inch piece of green thread, and then
thread the needle. Tie a double knot near the
other end of the thread.

6. Whipstitch the leaves to the apple. To whipstitch, come up at A and stitch over the edge of the leaf to go down at B.

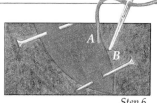

Step 6

7. Come up at C. Keep whipstitching all around the leaves. When you finish stitching, tie a knot underneath the felt close to your last stitch and cut off the extra thread. Then remove the pins.

Step 7

8. Place the apple shape without leaves onto the table. Lay the circle of batting on top. Place the other apple shape, leaf-side up, on top of the batting. Pin the edges together.

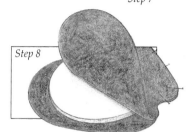

Step 8

9. Cut an 18-inch piece of red thread, and then thread the needle. Tie a double knot near the other end of the thread.

10. Whipstitch the apple shapes together as shown, starting at the top of the apple. Keep whipstitching until you have 1 inch left to stitch. Make a loop with the brown yarn and slip the ends between the felt.

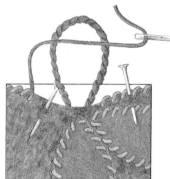

Step 10

11. Finish whipstitching the edge. Your stitches will hold the loop in place. Then remove the pins, and your potholder is complete! ★

THE BIG APPLE CRAZE

In the 1940s, "apple mania" swept the nation. People even learned a new dance called the Big Apple. These two women are demonstrating the dance while wearing dresses made from apple-print fabric!

SCOTTIE BOOKMARK

This playful pup will be happy to hold your place in your favorite book.

MATERIALS

Pencil
Sheet of tracing paper
Scissors
Straight pins
2 pieces of black felt, each 3 inches square
Black thread
Needle
10 inches of plaid ribbon, $\frac{1}{2}$ inch wide
Cotton ball
White glue
2 small plastic eyes

DIRECTIONS

1. Use the pencil to trace the Scottie dog pattern shown on page 43 onto tracing paper twice. Cut the patterns out.

2. Pin 1 Scottie pattern to each piece of felt. Cut out the Scottie dogs and unpin the patterns.

Step 2

3. Place 1 felt Scottie dog on top of the other and pin them together.

4. Cut an 18-inch piece of thread, and then thread the needle. Tie a double knot near the other end of the thread.

5. Whipstitch the Scottie dogs together. Starting at the back of the neck, bring the needle up at A and then pull the thread over the edge to come up at B.

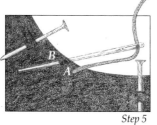

Step 5

6. Continue stitching around the edge of the Scottie dog until you've finished the tail. Then tie a knot close to your last stitch and cut off the extra thread.

7. Slip about $\frac{1}{2}$ inch of the plaid ribbon inside the Scottie dog. Then tuck a cotton ball inside the Scottie dog.

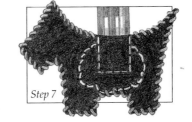

Step 7

8. Finish whipstitching the edge. Your stitches will hold the ribbon in place.

9. Glue 1 plastic eye onto each side of the Scottie dog's head.

10. Cut a "V" into the other end of the plaid ribbon, and your Scottie bookmark is finished! ★

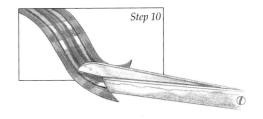

Step 10

A Scottie dog button.

SCOTTIE DOGS

Scottish terriers, or "Scotties," are a breed of dog from Scotland. In Molly's time, President Franklin D. Roosevelt, shown at left, had a pet Scottie named Fala (FAH-lah) that became a national mascot. Scottie dogs were popular as toys and on clothes, bookmarks, place mats, and buttons.

PHOTO HOLDER

Molly made photo holders to
carry pictures of her friends and
to send to soldiers overseas.

MATERIALS

2 felt rectangles, each 3 by 4 inches
Ruler
Fabric pen
Scissors
Felt rectangle, $6\frac{1}{4}$ by 4 inches
Straight pins
Thread
Needle
2 pieces of clear plastic, each $2\frac{3}{4}$ by $3\frac{1}{2}$ inches*
Snapshots of your family or friends
2 pieces of poster board, each $2\frac{3}{4}$ by $3\frac{1}{2}$ inches
*Available in art supply stores, or you can use
 the clear plastic from report covers.

DIRECTIONS

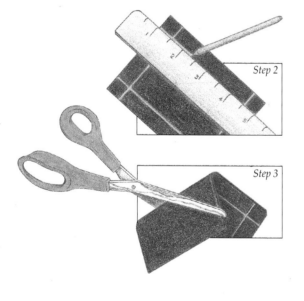

Step 2

Step 3

1. Lay a small felt rectangle onto a table.

2. To make a frame, use the ruler and fabric pen
to draw a line $\frac{1}{2}$ inch from each edge of the
rectangle.

3. Cut out the center rectangle. To begin cutting,
fold the felt in half. Then cut a slit on the fold.
Unfold the felt, and continue cutting.

4. Make a frame from the other small felt
rectangle in the same way.

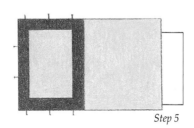

Step 5

5. Lay the large felt rectangle onto the table.
Then lay 1 of the frame pieces on top, with
the *right side*, or front side, facing up. Pin
3 edges together.

6. Cut an 18-inch piece of thread, and then thread the needle. Tie a double knot near the other end of the thread.

7. Whipstitch around the 3 pinned edges. To whipstitch, come up at A. Then stitch over the edge of the felt to come up at B.

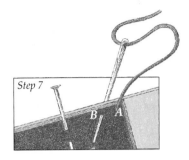

Step 7

8. When you've finished stitching, tie a knot close to your last stitch and cut off the extra thread.

Step 8

9. Sew the other frame piece to the large felt rectangle in the same way. Remove the pins.

10. Slide the clear plastic into the frames, and then add snapshots of your family and friends. Slip the poster board rectangles behind the snapshots to add support to your photo holder. ★

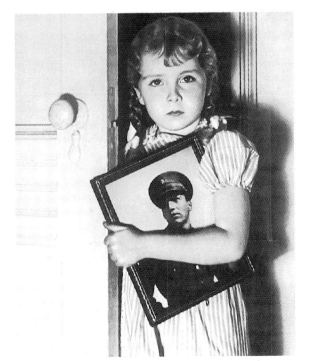

PRECIOUS PICTURES

Before soldiers were shipped out, they often took pictures of their families and friends. When soldiers were lonely, those pictures brought back happy memories. Many soldiers had pictures taken of themselves, too, so families and friends would have something to remember them by.

RAINY DAY FUN

Illustration by Nick Backes

Molly woke up to the steady *plip plop plip plop* of rain on her bedroom window. *Not on a Saturday!* she thought as she covered her head with her blanket, just like a turtle pulling its head back into its shell. Then she remembered. Saturday was movie day!

At the movies, it didn't matter if it was rainy outside. Inside the theater, everything seemed exciting and magical. The theater was like a palace, with plush velvet seats and glittering chandeliers. For only 25 cents, Molly saw a full-length movie plus cartoons and newsreels that showed war events. And popcorn and candy were only a nickel each!

After the movie, Molly and her friends Linda and Susan puddle-jumped to Molly's house. Molly's mom worked at the Red Cross on Saturday afternoons, but Mrs. Gilford was there to keep an eye on them. Sometimes Mrs. Gilford even had good ideas for curing the rainy day blues.

One afternoon she taught the girls how to carve soap. Molly made soap fish and arranged them in a basket to give Mom for her birthday. Mrs. Gilford also taught them how to play a game called Handshake. The girls took turns tossing bean-filled gloves onto the game board and trying to make them "shake hands" in the middle square.

The girls also spent rainy afternoons reading Bugs Bunny and Donald Duck comic books and listening to radio shows. Linda and Susan liked to listen to "The Lone Ranger," but Molly liked "Wonder Woman" best. Wonder Woman had a magic golden lasso, an invisible airplane, and, best of all, she was the only woman superhero on the radio!

RAINY DAY FUN

Soap Fish

•

Handshake Game

•

Corral Bookends

WHAT ABOUT TELEVISION?

In 1944, most people had never seen a television set! Only a very few television sets were made before the war, and then factories stopped making them until the war was over. After the war, many families like the one shown here bought television sets, even though the pictures were only in black and white.

SOAP FISH

*A school of soap fish will make
a colorful splash in your bath!*

MATERIALS

Pencil
Piece of tracing paper, 5 inches square
Scissors
Manicure stick*
2 cakes of soap, any colors *(Glycerine soaps work well.)*
Tissues for polishing
2 thumbtacks
Soap dish, basket, and bath beads *(optional)*
Available in the cosmetics section of department stores.

DIRECTIONS

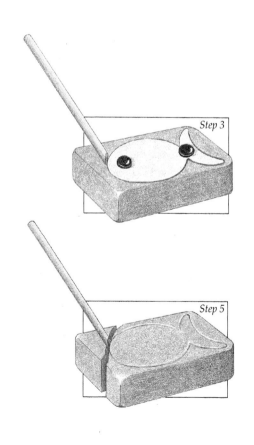

1. Use the pencil to trace the fish pattern shown on page 43 onto tracing paper, and then cut it out.

2. Use the side of the manicure stick to scrape any lettering from the sides of the soap cakes. Then rub the sides with tissues or your fingers so you'll have a smooth surface for carving.

3. Lay the fish pattern on top of 1 of the soap cakes. Push 1 thumbtack through the body of the fish and another thumbtack through the tail.

4. Trace around the pattern with the manicure stick. Remove the thumbtacks and pattern.

5. Use the point of the manicure stick to carve away the soap around the fish outline, a little at a time.

6. Round the edges of the soap fish with the side of the manicure stick.

Step 3

Step 5

7. Continue carving the fish until you are happy with its shape.

8. Use the point of the manicure stick to add eyes, a mouth, and scales.

9. Polish your soap fish by rubbing it with tissues or your fingers.

10. Then make another soap fish in the same way. Keep them in a soap dish to brighten your bathroom.

11. Try carving other shapes, too. Arrange them in a basket, add a few bath beads, and give them as gifts! ★

SOAP SAVERS

When soap was in short supply, one way to s-t-r-e-t-c-h a family's soap supply was to save slivers of leftover soap and then press them together in a soap saver to make a bigger bar. Families also let their soap sit in water to make liquid soap.

WASHING CLOTHES

In Molly's time, washing clothes was more work than it is today. Electric washers had tubs where soapy water was swished through clothes, just like today's washers. But then each piece of clothing had to be run through a wringer by hand. The **wringer** *is the set of rollers at the top of the washer shown here.*

HANDSHAKE GAME

It takes good aim to get these gloves to "shake hands" in the middle of the board!

MATERIALS

Sheet of poster board, 30 inches square
Pencil
Yardstick
Foam paintbrush, 1 inch wide
Acrylic paints, any colors
Thick black marking pen
2 cloth gloves
4 cups of dried beans
2 rubber bands

DIRECTIONS

1. To make the game board, lay the square of poster board onto the floor.

2. Use the pencil and yardstick to mark 2 dots on 1 side of the square, 10 inches apart. Mark the other 3 sides of the square in the same way.

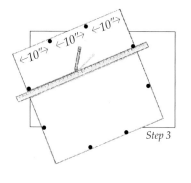

Step 3

3. Line up your yardstick along 2 dots that are across from each other. Draw a pencil line to connect the 2 dots.

4. Connect the rest of the dots in the same way. You will end up with a grid of 10-inch squares.

5. Use the foam paintbrush to paint the center square any color you like.

6. When the paint is dry, paint the outer squares another color. Your pencil lines should still show through the paint.

7. When the paint is dry, use the black marking pen and ruler to trace over your pencil lines.

8. Fill the gloves with dried beans. Then close the wrists of the gloves with rubber bands.

Step 8

9. When your game board is dry, you're ready to play Handshake. You can play with as many friends as you like.

10. Each player stands 5 feet from the game board and then tosses the gloves 1 at a time onto the game board.

11. Count 5 points each time the gloves touch, or "shake hands," in the middle square. Count 1 point if the gloves touch in any of the outer squares. ★

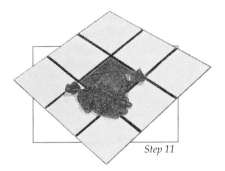

Step 11

PATRIOTIC BOARD GAMES

One of Molly's favorite games was called "Get In the Scrap." It followed a truckload of scrap metal from the time it was collected until it was melted to make war supplies. The game urged Molly to get out and collect scrap, too. The directions said, "Get In the Scrap— Play it! Do it!"

CORRAL BOOKENDS

Fence in your favorite books!

WESTERNS

In the 1940s, movies called Westerns made stars like John Wayne and Roy Rogers into American heroes. These actors played cowboys who defeated the bandits every time. Children often wore Western clothes, and they loved anything with a Western theme, from bedspreads to book bags!

MATERIALS

Small artist's paintbrush
Acrylic paint *(white and green)*
8 craft sticks
Fine sandpaper (150 grit)
2 wood blocks, each 5 inches long, 3 inches wide, and 1½ inches thick*
Foam paintbrush, 1 inch wide
Ruler
White glue
Any of the following: miniature animals, flowers, farm tools, and hay bales
**Available in hardware and lumber stores.*

DIRECTIONS

1. Use the artist's paintbrush to paint 1 side of each craft stick white.

2. When the paint is dry, turn over the craft sticks and paint the other sides. Paint the edges, too. Give the craft sticks another coat of white paint if necessary.

3. Rub sandpaper over the sides and edges of the blocks of wood until they are smooth. Brush away the dust.

4. Use the foam paintbrush to paint 1 side of each wood block green. Let the paint dry, and then paint another side.

5. Keep painting until all the sides are green. Give the wood blocks another coat of green paint if necessary.

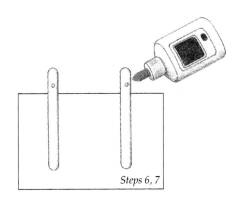

6. To make the fence, lay 2 craft sticks onto a table, about 3 inches apart. These will be your fence posts.

Steps 6, 7

7. Squeeze a tiny dot of glue about ¾ inch down from the top of each fence post.

8. Lay another craft stick across the glue on the fence posts. This is the top rail of your fence.

9. Squeeze another tiny dot of glue onto each fence post, about 1 inch down from the top rail. Lay another craft stick across the glue. You've finished the fence!

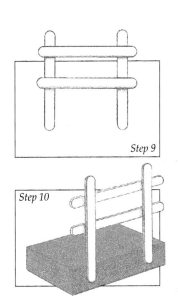

Step 9

Step 10

10. When the glue on the fence is dry, squeeze a little glue on the bottom of each fence post. Glue the fence to 1 of the wood blocks as shown.

11. Repeat steps 6 through 10 to build another fence and attach it to the second wood block.

12. Glue on miniature animals, flowers, farm tools, and hay bales, and your bookends are finished! ★

ODDS AND ENDS

Empty toothpaste tubes were made into war supplies, too!

Duringcare of their belongings to make them last.
They couldn't get many new clothes, shoes, or toys because most factories were making only war supplies. Since families couldn't get new things until after the war, they tried hard not to waste anything!

Mrs. Gilford made sure that almost nothing went to waste in the McIntire household. One of her favorite sayings was, "Use it up, wear it out, make it do, or do without." Even when things seemed to be all used up or worn out, Mrs. Gilford still wouldn't throw them away. She saved them in a scrap box in the hall closet.

The scrap box was a jumble of all sorts of odds and ends—bits of rickrack saved from worn-out dresses, tangled yarn, stray buttons, and scraps of faded fabric. There was even tissue paper from last year's Christmas gifts. Mrs. Gilford had uncrumpled it and carefully folded it into neat squares.

Ricky usually called the scrap box the "nothing" box. He said there was nothing in it that was any good. But Molly thought it was a box of possibilities. She loved to think of ways to make something from all that "nothing."

Molly used buttons and rickrack from the scrap box to decorate pictures of her favorite movie stars, like Ava Gardner and Hedy Lamarr. She found some flower-shaped buttons to make a bouquet for Ava Gardner and some tiny white buttons to make a pearl necklace for Hedy Lamarr.

Molly found a way to use the Christmas tissue paper, too. She glued small pieces of the paper onto a glass jar. The jar was perfect for holding pencils, and when Molly held it up to the light, it looked like a stained-glass window.

ODDS AND ENDS

Leather-Topped Box

•

Scrap-Paper Jar

•

Button Collage

SCRAP DRIVES

Everyone on the home front was encouraged to save old metal and rubber. Children collected bottle caps, metal cans, old tires, and foil wrappers from chewing gum. Children even gave their metal toys to scrap drives!

LEATHER-TOPPED BOX

Stamp your own designs to create a beautiful box for your dresser top!

MATERIALS

Fine sandpaper (150 grit)
Wooden box with lid, 4 inches square
Foam paintbrush, 1 inch wide
Acrylic paint, any color
Sponge
Small bowl of water
Scrap of tooling leather for practice*
2 or 3 leather-craft stamping tools*
Small wooden mallet*
Pencil
Piece of paper, 3½ inches square
Piece of tooling leather, 3½ inches square*
White glue

Available in leather-supply stores and craft stores. Look under "Leather Supplies" in the yellow pages of the phone book.

DIRECTIONS

1. Lightly sand the wooden box and lid. Wipe away the dust.

2. Use the foam paintbrush to paint the box and lid any color you like.

3. Let the paint dry for about 15 minutes. Add a second coat if necessary. Set the box and lid aside to dry.

4. Dip the sponge into the bowl of water. Squeeze out some of the water.

5. Use the sponge to dampen first the rough side of the scrap leather and then the smooth side.

Step 5

6. Lay the scrap leather, rough side down, onto a sturdy table or workbench.

7. Try out your stamping tools. Hold a tool upright, with the design end resting on the leather.

8. Ask an adult to help you strike the stamping tool with the mallet. A firm tap is usually enough for small stamping tools. You may want to tap several times when you use a large stamping tool.

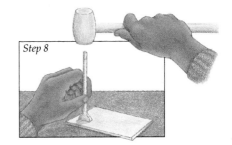

Step 8

9. Plan your design. You might want to pencil a rough design onto the paper square before you begin stamping the leather square.

10. When you're happy with your design, use the sponge to dampen first the rough side of the leather square and then the smooth side.

11. Stamp your design onto the leather square just as you've practiced.

12. If the leather gets too dry, dampen it again and continue stamping until your design is finished.

13. Then glue the leather square, design side up, to the top of the box lid. Your box is finished! ★

SHOE SHORTAGES

Sometimes leather for shoes was in short supply during the war. Shoe factories needed to make boots for soldiers instead of sneakers and dress-up shoes for home-front families. Children like Molly often wore hand-me-down shoes when they couldn't get new ones.

SCRAP-PAPER JAR

Molly liked this jar because it was both pretty and practical.

MATERIALS

Scissors
Tissue paper, any colors
Ruler
White glue
Small bowl
Foam paintbrush, 1 inch wide
Glass jar

DIRECTIONS

1. Cut the tissue paper into small shapes, about $\frac{1}{2}$ inch wide.

2. Squeeze a little glue into the bowl. Wet the foam paintbrush, and then dip it into the glue. Brush the glue onto the jar until you've covered an area about 3 inches square.

Step 3

3. Place the tissue-paper shapes onto the glue. Overlap them so no glass shows through. Continue pasting tissue-paper shapes onto the jar until the whole jar is covered. If the brush gets sticky, wet it again.

4. Let the glue dry, and then give the whole jar a top coat of glue. The glue will look milky at first, but it will dry clear. ★

WARTIME PAPER

Even though paper was sometimes scarce on the home front, the government made sure that newspapers and magazines that published war news had enough paper. And book publishers saved paper by making books with smaller type so more words could fit on each page.

BUTTON COLLAGE

MATERIALS

White glue
Photograph or magazine picture, 5 by 6 inches
Piece of poster board, 5 by 6 inches
Small, flat buttons in assorted colors, shapes,
  and sizes
Rickrack, any color

*Decorate a special picture
with beautiful buttons!*

DIRECTIONS

1. Glue the picture to the poster board. Smooth out any air bubbles with your fingers.

2. Plan your design. Think about what parts of the picture you'd like to decorate with buttons, and what colors and shapes of buttons will look best.

3. Try out your design. Arrange your buttons until you are happy with how they look. Try layering your buttons for a three-dimensional effect.

Step 3

4. Glue the buttons onto your picture. For a finishing touch, glue on a colorful border of rickrack. ★

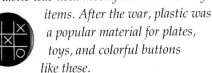

**FANTASTIC
PLASTIC**

*Plastic was called a "miracle of modern
science" in the 1940s. During the war,
plastic was used mostly to make military
items. After the war, plastic was
a popular material for plates,
toys, and colorful buttons
like these.*

PATTERNS

STAR WHIRLER

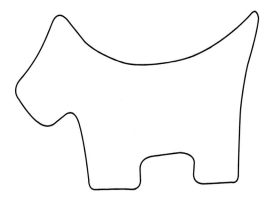

SCOTTIE BOOKMARK

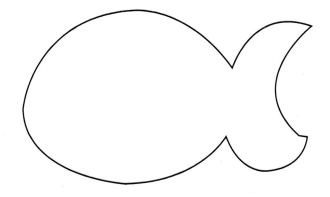

SOAP FISH

STAR STAMP

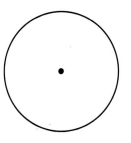

PINWHEEL CIRCLE

APPLE POTHOLDER